|| Dedicated to Wisdom Seekers Around The World ||

ECHOES OF ANCIENT WISDOM

EXPLORING THE RICH HERITAGE OF INDIAN SPIRITUALITY

DR. JAGADEESH PILLAI

Contents

Prayer   *vii*

About The Author   *ix*

Preface   *xiii*

1. The Roots Of Indian Spirituality: An Introduction To   1
   The Vedas And Upanishads

Part 1

2. Journey To The East: Exploring The Origins And   7
   Development Of Yoga

Part 2

3. The Many Paths To Enlightenment: An Overview Of   13
   The Different Schools Of Indian Spirituality

Part 3

4. "the Bhagavad Gita: A Guide To The Path Of Action   19
   And Devotion"

Part 4

5. The Upanishads: Uncovering The Secrets Of The   25
   Inner Self

Part 5

6. The Ramayana: A Cultural And Spiritual Exploration 31
   Of A Timeless Epic

Part 6

7. The Mahabharata: An In-depth Look At One Of   37
   India's Greatest Spiritual Texts

Part 7

Contents

8. The Impact Of Buddhism On Indian Spirituality   43

Part 8

9. Meditation And Mindfulness: Techniques And   49

Practices For Cultivating Inner Peace

Part 9

10. From Temples To Ashrams: A Guide To The Sacred   55

Places Of Indian Spirituality

Part 10

11. The Future Of Indian Spirituality: Contemporary   61

Trends And Challenges

Part 11

12. Rivers Of Faith: The Sacred Rivers Of India And   67

Their Connection To Spiritual Traditions And Beliefs

Part 12

13. Quotes From Indian Scriptures   73

Part 13

14. Summary   79

Part 14

Other Books Of The Author   83

Contact   87

Prayer

"Om Poornamadah Poornamidam Poornat
Poornamudachyate,Poornasya Poornamaadaya
Poornamevavashishyate,Om Shantih, Shantih, Shantih"

*The literal interpretation of this mantra is: That which is
Absolute, This which is Absolute, Absolute arises from Absolute,
If Absolute is removed from Absolute, Absolute remains
OM Peace, Peace, Peace.*

ᕖᕖᕖ

About The Author

Dr. Jagadeesh Pillai is a renowned Guinness World Record holder, writer, and researcher hailing from Varanasi, also known as the abode of Lord Shiva. With a Ph.D. in Vedic Science and a range of creative ideas and achievements, he is a true polymath. He is the author of more than 100 books including Research Publications. Although his roots can be traced back to Kerala, the people of Varanasi hold him in high regard and affectionately consider him one of their own.

Dr. Pillai has achieved four Guinness World Records in the following subjects:

"Script to Screen" - In this record, Dr. Pillai produced and directed an animation film within the shortest time possible, breaking the previous record set by Canadians. He has also received numerous national and international awards and recognitions for this achievement.

Longest Line of Postcards - For this record, Dr. Pillai created a line of 16,300 postcards on the occasion of the 163rd anniversary of Indian Postal Day. The event also included a questionnaire about the Indian flag.

Largest Poster Awareness Campaign - Dr. Pillai designed an awareness campaign on the subject of "Beti Bachao - Beti Padhao" (Save the Girl Child - Educate the Girl Child) to achieve this record.

Largest Envelope - In tribute to the Indian Prime Minister's

"Make in India" initiative, Dr. Pillai created a 4000 square meter envelope using waste paper to achieve this record.

Attempted - **70000 Candles on a 210 kg Cake** - To celebrate the 70th Indian Independence Day, Dr. Pillai attempted to light 70,000 candles on a 210 kg cake, which was recorded in World Records India.

Attempted - **Documentary on Dhamek Stupa of Sarnath in 17 Languages** - Dr. Pillai attempted to create a documentary on the Dhamek Stupa of Sarnath, dubbing it in 17 different languages. The result of this attempt is currently awaiting confirmation from the Guinness World Records.

Dr. Pillai is skilled in teaching the Bhagavad Gita, a Hindu scripture, and is popular among young people. He has helped many young people improve their lives through his motivational teachings.

In addition to teaching, he has composed and sung numerous Sanskrit Bhajans and patriotic songs.

He has also written and directed several short films and documentaries for awareness campaigns, and has volunteered with the police in both UP and Kerala to spread awareness about various issues through videos and photography.

Incredibly, he has produced and directed over 100 documentaries about the city of Varanasi, all on his own.

He has also helped and guided more than 25 boys and girls to achieve world records through creative and innovative methods. He is a multifaceted person who uses his intellect and the blessings given to him by God to excel in various areas. He is both a teacher and a student, always learning and teaching, and is able to master any subject he comes across.

He is a selfless social activist and motivational speaker who has overcome struggles and failures to become a successful and enthusiastic individual with a rich life experience.

In addition to his work with the Bhagavad Gita, he is also an efficient Tarot card reader, Astro-Vastu consultant, and a talented singer and composer. He has sung the entire Ram Charita Manas and Bhagavad Gita in his own compositions, and has sung the phrase "Lokah Samastha Sukhino Bhavantu" in 50 different languages. He is currently working on a detailed and scientific study of Vedas, Upanishads, Puranas, and the Bhagavad Gita. He has also composed and sung the Hanuman Chalisa and Gayatri Mantra in 108 and 1008 different compositions, respectively.

Awards - Four Times Guinness World Records, Winner of Mahatma Gandhi Vishwa Shanti Puraskar, Mahatma Gandhi Global Peace Ambassador, Kashi Ratna Award, Dr. APJ Abdul Kalam Motivational Person of the Year 2017, Mother Teresa Award, Indira Gandhi Priyadarshini Award, Bharat Vikas Ratna Award, Udyog Ratna Award, Vigyan Prasar Award, Poorvanchal Ratn Samman.

ॐॐॐ

Preface

"Echoes of Ancient Wisdom: Exploring the Rich Heritage of Indian Spirituality" is a comprehensive guide to the diverse spiritual traditions and practices that have been a part of Indian culture and heritage for thousands of years. This book delves into the complex and rich world of Indian spirituality, exploring its origins, development and contemporary trends.

The book begins with an introduction to the Vedas and Upanishads, the ancient texts that form the foundation of Indian spiritual thought. We then move on to explore the origins and development of Yoga and the many paths to enlightenment offered by the different schools of Indian spirituality. We also take an in-depth look at some of India's greatest spiritual texts such as the Bhagavad Gita, The Ramayana, The Mahabharata and Upanishads.

The book also explores the impact of Buddhism on Indian spirituality, providing a detailed account of the principles and practices that distinguish it from the traditional spiritual traditions of India. Meditation and mindfulness are also explored, offering techniques and practices for cultivating inner peace. Finally, the book offers a guide to the sacred places of Indian spirituality, including temples and ashrams, and the challenges and trends affecting Indian spirituality today and the future.

This book is written for anyone with an interest in Indian spirituality and its rich cultural heritage, it is suitable for people of all backgrounds and spiritual inclinations. It provides a detailed and accessible introduction to the concepts and practices of Indian spirituality, and a deeper understanding of one of the most ancient and profound spiritual traditions in the world.

We hope that this book will serve as a valuable resource for those seeking to gain a deeper understanding of Indian spirituality, its rich history and its ongoing relevance in today's world. Whether you are a student of spiritual studies, a practitioner of yoga or meditation, or simply someone with a curiosity about the spiritual traditions of India, this book has something to offer. It is an invitation to embark on a journey of discovery, where you will gain insight into the timeless wisdom of ancient Indian spirituality and its ongoing relevance to our lives today.

Through the detailed and engaging examination of each subject matter, this book aims to offer readers an appreciation of the complexities and richness of the Indian spiritual heritage and its ongoing relevance today. It is our hope that "Echoes of Ancient Wisdom" will be a valuable resource for anyone interested in understanding the depth and beauty of Indian spirituality.

ᐅᐅᐅ

ONE

THE ROOTS OF INDIAN SPIRITUALITY: AN INTRODUCTION TO THE VEDAS AND UPANISHADS

Indian spirituality has a rich and ancient history that can be traced back to the Vedas and Upanishads. The Vedas, which are considered the oldest sacred texts of Hinduism, date back to around 1500 BCE. They consist of four collections of hymns, prayers, and liturgical formulas that were passed down orally for centuries before being written down. The Upanishads, which are considered to be the end portion of the Vedas, were written around 800-600 BCE. They contain the core teachings and philosophy of Vedanta, which is one of the six traditional schools of Indian philosophy.

The Vedas are divided into four collections, known as the Rigveda, Yajurveda, Samaveda, and Atharvaveda. The Rigveda is the oldest and most important of the Vedas, and it contains hymns to various deities, as well as rituals and religious instructions. The Yajurveda contains liturgical formulas for performing yajna (sacrifices), while the Samaveda contains hymns and chants that were used during the performance of yajna. The Atharvaveda is a collection of spells, charms, and incantations used for healing and protection.

The Upanishads are considered to be the spiritual heart of the Vedas, and they contain the core teachings and philosophy of Indian spirituality. They present the idea of Brahman, the ultimate reality and consciousness, and the Atman, the individual soul, as one and the same, and in the unity with it is the goal of human existence. They explain the idea of karma, the law of cause and effect, and discuss the nature of reality, including the concepts of maya (illusion) and samsara (reincarnation). They also discuss the path to liberation, known as moksha, which is achieved through the realization of the unity of Atman and Brahman.

One of the key Upanishads is the Bhagavad Gita, which is a part of the Mahabharata, one of the major Indian epic. Bhagavad Gita is a conversation between prince Arjuna and Lord Krishna, where Lord Krishna explains the nature of the ultimate reality, the role of self-less actions and importance of devotion in attaining the ultimate truth. It is considered as a central text of Hinduism, and it is widely studied and commented upon.

The Vedas and Upanishads form the foundation of Indian spirituality and have had a profound influence on the development of Hinduism, Buddhism, and Jainism. The concepts and teachings found in these texts continue to be studied and practiced by spiritual seekers in India and around the world today. They provide valuable insights into the nature of reality, the human condition, and the path to liberation.

In short, the Vedas and Upanishads form the foundation of Indian spirituality and have had a profound influence on the development of Hinduism, Buddhism, and Jainism. They contain the core teachings and philosophy of Vedanta which is one of the six traditional schools of Indian philosophy, and discuss the path to liberation which is achieved through the realization of the unity of Atman and Brahman. The Upanishads has a significant text Bhagavad Gita, which is a conversation between prince Arjuna and Lord Krishna and is considered as a central text of Hinduism.

ᴘᴘᴘ

"You are what your deep, driving desire is. As your desire is, so is your will. As your will is, so is your deed. As your deed is, so is your destiny." - The Upanishads

TWO

JOURNEY TO THE EAST: EXPLORING THE ORIGINS AND DEVELOPMENT OF YOGA

Yoga is an ancient spiritual practice that originated in India more than 5,000 years ago. The word "yoga" comes from the Sanskrit word "yuj," which means "to unite or join." In the context of yoga, it refers to the union of the individual consciousness with the universal consciousness.

The origins of yoga can be traced back to the Indus Valley Civilization, where seals depicting figures in yoga-like postures have been found. The earliest written record of yoga is in the Upanishads, a collection of texts that form the foundation of Vedantic philosophy. These texts discuss the concept of yoga as a means of attaining liberation from the cycle of reincarnation.

The Yoga Sutras of Patanjali, which were written around 400 CE, provide a comprehensive system of yoga. The text describes the eight limbs of yoga, also known as Ashtanga Yoga, which includes ethical principles, physical postures, breathing techniques, and meditation. The ultimate goal of this system is to achieve the state of enlightenment, known as samadhi.

Yoga was traditionally passed down through an oral tradition, with teachings passed down from teacher to student. However, in the 19th and early 20th centuries, yoga began to be more widely disseminated through the writings of figures such as Swami Vivekananda, who brought yoga to the West and helped to popularize it as a form of physical exercise and stress management.

In the late 20th century, Yoga becomes increasingly popular in Western countries, and various forms of yoga, such as Hatha, Vinyasa, and Kundalini, have evolved, along with its commercialization. Today, yoga is practiced all over the world, and it is widely recognized for its physical, mental and spiritual benefits. Yoga has been integrated into different field such as health, education, therapy, and sports for its therapeutic and holistic approach.

In conclusion, Yoga is an ancient spiritual practice that originated in India more than 5,000 years ago. The origins of yoga can be traced back to the Indus Valley Civilization and discussed in Upanishads. The Yoga Sutras of Patanjali provided a comprehensive system of yoga that include ethical principles, physical postures, breathing techniques, and meditation, with the ultimate goal of achieving enlightenment. Yoga was traditionally passed down through an oral tradition, but in 19th and early 20th centuries it began to be more widely disseminated. Today, yoga is practiced all over the world and it is widely recognized for its physical, mental and spiritual benefits, and integrated into various field.

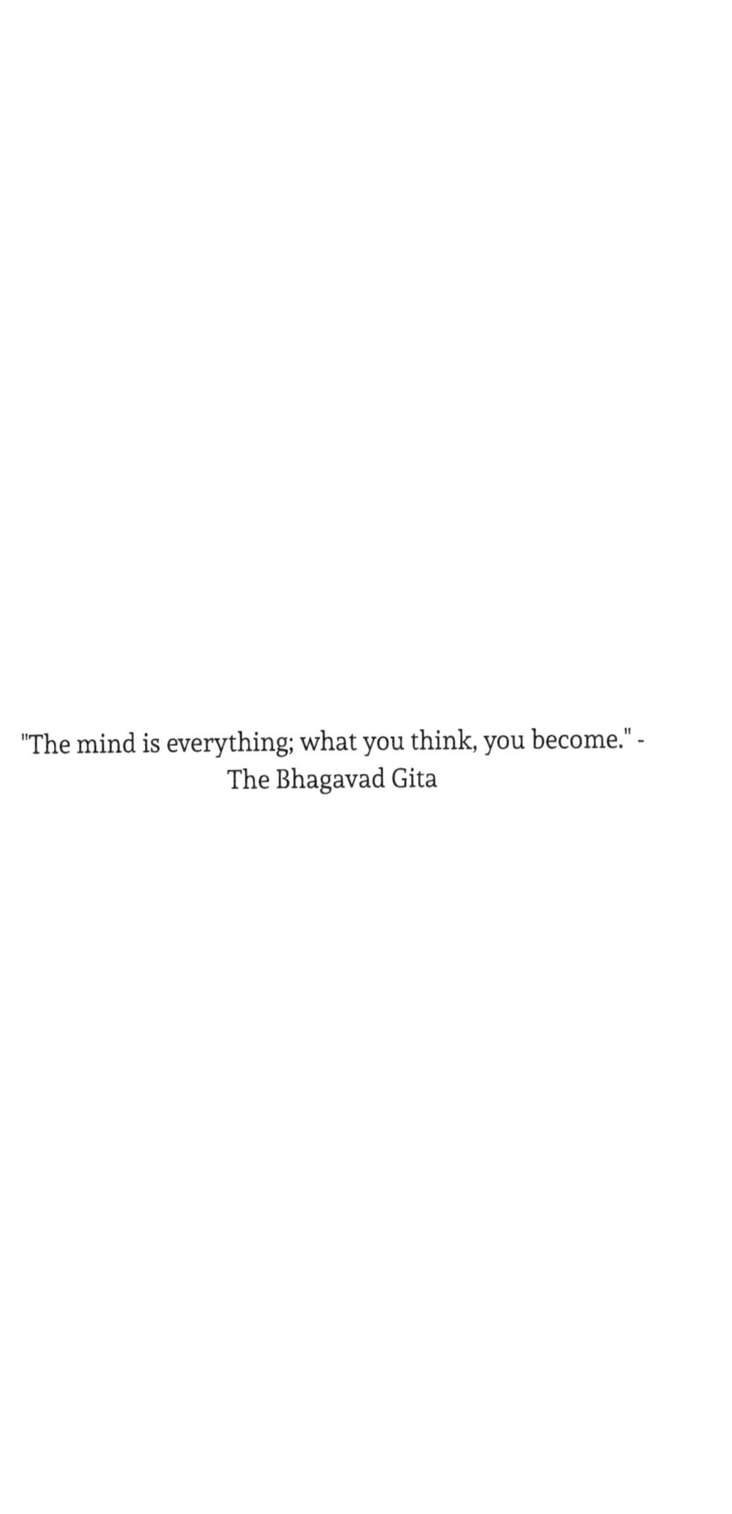

"The mind is everything; what you think, you become." - The Bhagavad Gita

THREE

The Many Paths to Enlightenment: An Overview of the Different Schools of Indian Spirituality

Indian spirituality has a rich and diverse tradition that encompasses many different schools of thought and practice. These schools, known as darshanas in Sanskrit, provide different paths and approaches to the ultimate goal of enlightenment, or moksha.

One of the major schools of Indian spirituality is Vedanta, which is based on the teachings of the Upanishads, and provide a non-dualistic understanding of ultimate reality as Brahman and the individual soul, or Atman, being one and the same. The Advaita Vedanta, one of the sub-school of Vedanta, is the most prominent and widely followed of Vedantic traditions and states that one can attain liberation through self-knowledge, direct experience and the realization of the identity of Atman and Brahman.

Another major school is Samkhya, which is one of the oldest systems of Indian philosophy and provides a dualistic understanding of ultimate reality. It posits the existence of two eternal realities: Purusha and Prakriti. Purusha is the consciousness and Prakriti is the matter. It emphasizes the practical means of attaining liberation through the discriminative knowledge of these two realities.

Yoga, which is often associated with physical postures and breathing techniques, is also considered a separate school. The Yoga school posits the existence of eight spiritual practices, or limbs, which lead to the attainment of the ultimate goal of samadhi or enlightenment.

Another school is the Mimamsa, which focuses on the study of the Vedas and the performance of Vedic rituals as the means of attaining liberation. It stresses the importance of right action in attaining liberation and emphasizes the importance of adhering to the laws of karma.

Buddhism and Jainism, while not considered traditional Indian darshanas, also have roots in ancient Indian spirituality and have had a significant influence on the development of Indian thought. Buddhism, which originated in India, emphasizes the attainment of enlightenment through the elimination of desire and suffering, while Jainism emphasizes the attainment of liberation through the cultivation of self-control and non-violence.

In short, Indian spirituality has a rich and diverse tradition that encompasses many different schools of thought and practice. The major ones being Vedanta, Samkhya, Yoga, Mimamsa and with Buddhism and Jainism having a significant influence on the development of Indian thought. Each of these schools provide different paths and approaches to the ultimate goal of enlightenment, or moksha, with some emphasizing on self-knowledge, others on right action, and some on the elimination of desire and suffering.

ppp

"The world is a mirror of the self. Your mind, your emotions, your actions, and your reactions create the world around you." - The Bhagavad Gita

FOUR

"THE BHAGAVAD GITA: A GUIDE TO THE PATH OF ACTION AND DEVOTION"

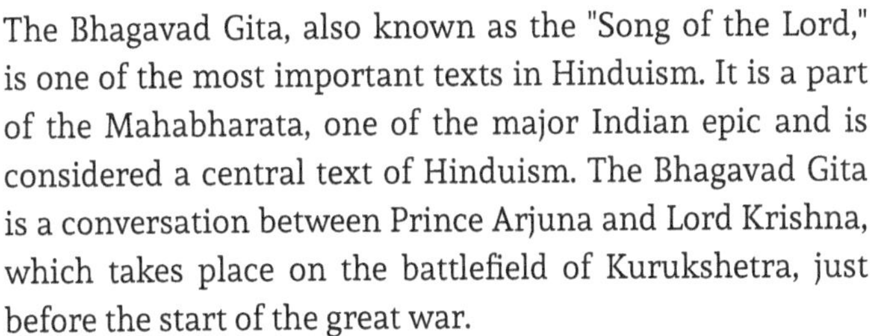

The Bhagavad Gita, also known as the "Song of the Lord," is one of the most important texts in Hinduism. It is a part of the Mahabharata, one of the major Indian epic and is considered a central text of Hinduism. The Bhagavad Gita is a conversation between Prince Arjuna and Lord Krishna, which takes place on the battlefield of Kurukshetra, just before the start of the great war.

The Bhagavad Gita presents a unique perspective on the nature of reality, the role of action, and the importance of devotion in attaining the ultimate goal of human existence, which is the realization of the self, or the Atman. It teaches that our actions should be performed as a service to God and that we should not be attached to the fruits of our actions.

One of the key teaching of Bhagavad Gita is the concept of Karma yoga, the path of action and selfless service. It explains that all actions should be performed without attachment to the results, and instead with the intent of offering the actions to God. This is the path to true freedom and liberation from the cycle of birth and death.

The Bhagavad Gita also teaches the importance of devotion, or Bhakti yoga, in attaining the ultimate goal of self-realization. It explains that true devotion is not just about performing external rituals or offerings but about developing a deep, personal relationship with God. It is through this devotional attitude that one can transcend the ego and connect with the divine.

Additionally, the Bhagavad Gita also discuss about the three main paths for attaining the ultimate goal which are Karma yoga, Bhakti yoga and Jnana yoga. Karma yoga is the path of action, Bhakti yoga is the path of devotion and Jnana yoga is the path of knowledge. It emphasizes that ultimately all paths lead to the same goal, which is the realization of the unity of Atman and Brahman.

The Bhagavad Gita is considered a central text of Hinduism and an important guide to the path of action and devotion. It presents a unique perspective on the nature of reality, the role of action and the importance of devotion in attaining the ultimate goal of human existence, which is the realization of the self or the Atman. It teaches the concept of Karma yoga, the path of action and selfless service, the importance of devotion or Bhakti yoga and the significance of the unity of Atman and Brahman. It is considered as a guide for people in all walks of life and for all times.

ϷϷϷ

"The one who sees the supreme Lord dwelling equally in all beings, and everywhere, never harms anyone." - Bhagavad Gita

FIVE

THE UPANISHADS: UNCOVERING THE SECRETS OF THE INNER SELF

The Upanishads are a collection of texts that are considered to be the end portion of the Vedas, the ancient sacred texts of Hinduism. They contain the core teachings and philosophy of Indian spirituality, and they are considered to be the spiritual heart of the Vedas. The Upanishads were written around 800-600 BCE, and they provide valuable insights into the nature of reality, the human condition, and the path to liberation.

One of the central teachings of the Upanishads is the concept of Brahman, which is the ultimate reality and consciousness. It is the ultimate, unchanging, and eternal reality that underlies and pervades the entire universe. The Upanishads also discuss the concept of Atman, which is the individual soul. They present the idea that Brahman and Atman are one and the same, and that the goal of human existence is to realize this unity.

The Upanishads also introduce the concept of Maya, which is the illusion of the world we perceive. It states that our experience of the world is not the ultimate reality, but rather an illusion created by our own ignorance. The Upanishads also discuss the concept of samsara, which is the cycle of reincarnation. They state that liberation, or moksha, can be attained through the realization of the unity of Atman and Brahman, and the attainment of Self-knowledge.

The Upanishads also describe the different paths to attain liberation, such as Jnana yoga, Karma yoga, and Bhakti yoga. Jnana yoga is the path of knowledge and self-enquiry, Karma yoga is the path of action and selfless service, and Bhakti yoga is the path of devotion and love towards the Divine. They emphasize that ultimate realization of the self, or Atman, can be achieved through any of these paths, and all paths ultimately lead to the same goal, liberation or moksha.

The Upanishads are considered the spiritual heart of the Vedas, the ancient sacred texts of Hinduism. They provide valuable insights into the nature of reality, the human condition, and the path to liberation. The Upanishads present the idea of Brahman and Atman being one and the same and the ultimate goal of human existence is to realize this unity. It also discuss about the concepts of Maya, Samsara and liberation, which can be attained through the self-knowledge. It also describes the different paths to attain liberation, such as Jnana yoga, Karma yoga, and Bhakti yoga and emphasize that ultimate realization of the self can be achieved through any of these paths.

ᑭᑭᑭ

"The supreme goal of life is the realization of the self, the
true self." - The Upanishads

SIX

THE RAMAYANA: A CULTURAL AND SPIRITUAL EXPLORATION OF A TIMELESS EPIC

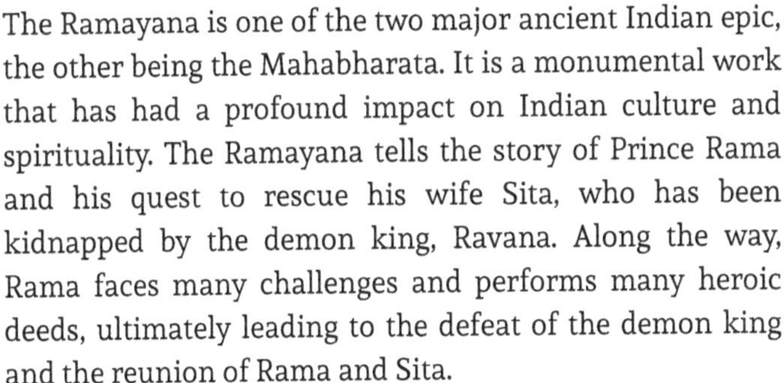

The Ramayana is one of the two major ancient Indian epic, the other being the Mahabharata. It is a monumental work that has had a profound impact on Indian culture and spirituality. The Ramayana tells the story of Prince Rama and his quest to rescue his wife Sita, who has been kidnapped by the demon king, Ravana. Along the way, Rama faces many challenges and performs many heroic deeds, ultimately leading to the defeat of the demon king and the reunion of Rama and Sita.

The Ramayana not only tells an exciting and dramatic

story, but it also explores important themes and concepts that are relevant to Indian spirituality and culture. One of the central themes is the concept of dharma, which is the moral and ethical code that guides the actions of all living beings. The story of Rama exemplifies the importance of adhering to dharma, even in difficult and challenging circumstances.

Another important theme is the concept of devotion and bhakti. The devotion of Rama's wife Sita, and his brother Lakshmana, and Hanuman, the monkey god, towards Rama is an important aspect of the story and exemplifies the deep devotion that is possible between a human and a god. Additionally, the story also portrays the devotion of Rama towards his duties, his family and his people.

The Ramayana also explores the concept of sacrifice, especially in the character of Rama, who is willing to sacrifice everything for the greater good, including his own happiness, for the sake of his family, people, and the adherence to dharma.

The Ramayana has had a tremendous impact on Indian culture and has been passed down through the generations in the form of storytelling, music, dance, and art. It is considered as an important text in Hinduism, and many temples and shrines are dedicated to the characters of the story. It is also considered as a guide for people in all walks of life and for all times, and the characters of the story are still widely revered today as models of virtue and righteousness.

The Ramayana is one of the two major ancient Indian epic

and is a monumental work that has had a profound impact on Indian culture and spirituality. It tells the story of Prince Rama and his quest to rescue his wife Sita, and along the way, it explores important themes and concepts that are relevant to Indian spirituality and culture, such as dharma, devotion, bhakti, sacrifice and also the nature of devotion, duty and righteousness. The Ramayana has been passed down through the generations and still widely revered as an important text in Hinduism and considered as a guide for people in all walks of life and for all times.

ᗑᗑᗑ

"The self is not the body, not the mind, not the ego, but the one who dwells within." - The Upanishads

SEVEN
THE MAHABHARATA: AN IN-DEPTH LOOK AT ONE OF INDIA'S GREATEST SPIRITUAL TEXTS

The Mahabharata is one of the two major ancient Indian epics, the other being the Ramayana. It is a vast and complex work that tells the story of a great war between the Kuru and Pandava dynasties, but also encompasses a wide range of themes and concepts that are central to Indian spirituality and culture.

One of the central themes of the Mahabharata is the concept of Dharma, which is the moral and ethical code that guides the actions of all living beings. The characters in the epic must navigate complex questions of duty and moral responsibility, highlighting the importance of adhering to one's Dharma even in the face of difficult and challenging circumstances.

The Mahabharata also explores the themes of Karma, the law of cause and effect, and the concept of the cycle of rebirth, or samsara. The characters in the epic must come to terms with the consequences of their actions, and the moral implications of their choices.

Another important theme in the Mahabharata is the concept of devotion and Bhakti. The text tells the story of the devotion of the main characters, such as Draupadi and the Pandavas, towards Lord Krishna, who is considered an incarnation of Vishnu, one of the major Hindu deities. It explores the nature of devotion, and how it can lead to liberation and self-realization.

One of the most famous parts of the Mahabharata is the Bhagavad Gita, which is a conversation between Prince Arjuna and Lord Krishna, where Lord Krishna explains the nature of the ultimate reality, the role of self-less actions and importance of devotion in attaining the ultimate truth. It is considered as a central text of Hinduism and is widely studied and commented upon.

The Mahabharata has had a tremendous impact on Indian culture and has been passed down through the generations in the form of storytelling, music, dance, and art. It is also considered as a valuable guide for people in all walks of life and for all times, and its teachings are still widely studied and applied in modern times. The characters and events of the epic are still widely revered and referenced in Indian culture, with many temples and shrines dedicated to the various deities and characters of the story.

The Mahabharata is one of the two major ancient Indian epic, a vast and complex work that tells the story of a great war between the Kuru and Pandava dynasties but also encompasses a wide range of themes and concepts that are central to Indian spirituality and culture. It explores themes such as Dharma, Karma, Samsara, devotion, Bhakti and also the nature of ultimate reality, the role of self-less actions and the importance of devotion in attaining the ultimate truth. The Mahabharata is considered as a valuable guide for people in all walks of life and for all times and its teachings and characters are still widely studied and applied in modern times.

ᐳᐳᐳ

"The one who has conquered the mind, the mind is their best friend. But for one who has failed to do so, their mind will remain the greatest enemy." - Bhagavad Gita

EIGHT

THE IMPACT OF BUDDHISM ON INDIAN SPIRITUALITY

Buddhism, which originated in India more than 2,500 years ago, has had a significant impact on Indian spirituality. The teachings of the Buddha, also known as the Dharma, provide a different perspective on the nature of reality and the path to liberation than that found in traditional Indian spiritual traditions such as Hinduism.

The Buddha, whose real name was Siddhartha Gautama, taught that the source of suffering is our attachment to worldly things, and the path to liberation is to let go of our attachments and desires. He also taught the Four Noble Truths, which state that suffering exists, that suffering arises from craving and attachment, that it is possible to end suffering, and that the path to the cessation of suffering is the Eightfold Path. This path includes right understanding, right intention, right speech, right action, right livelihood, right effort, right mindfulness and right concentration.

One of the major teachings of Buddhism is the concept of non-self or anatman. This teaching goes against the belief of Atman (individual self) in Hinduism and Jainism. It states that there is no permanent and unchanging self, but rather that the self is constantly changing and that our sense of self is an illusion.

Buddhism also provides an alternative path to liberation than that found in traditional Indian spiritual traditions such as Karma and rebirth. It states that liberation is attained through the attainment of enlightenment or Nirvana. And that the means to achieve this goal is the Eightfold Path, which is a Middle Path between extremes of self-indulgence and self-mortification.

Buddhism was widely adopted in India and it spread to other parts of the world, it had a significant impact on Indian culture, art and architecture. The Buddha's teachings had a profound impact on the development of Indian thought, influencing the development of various spiritual and philosophical schools such as Advaita Vedanta, and many aspects of Buddhism continue to be an important influence in modern India.

Buddhism, which originated in India more than 2,500 years ago, has had a significant impact on Indian spirituality. The teachings of the Buddha provide a different perspective on the nature of reality and the path to liberation.

❦❦❦

"A true spiritual master is one who has realized the truth and is able to guide others on the path to liberation." - The Upanishads

NINE

MEDITATION AND MINDFULNESS: TECHNIQUES AND PRACTICES FOR CULTIVATING INNER PEACE

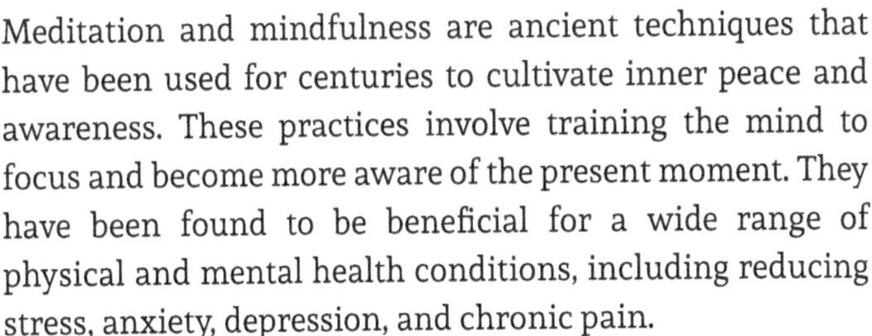

Meditation and mindfulness are ancient techniques that have been used for centuries to cultivate inner peace and awareness. These practices involve training the mind to focus and become more aware of the present moment. They have been found to be beneficial for a wide range of physical and mental health conditions, including reducing stress, anxiety, depression, and chronic pain.

There are many different types of meditation and

mindfulness techniques, each with their own unique focus and benefits. Some of the most popular and well-known practices include:

Transcendental Meditation (TM): This form of meditation involves the use of a mantra, or word or phrase, that is repeated silently to help focus the mind.

Mindfulness Meditation: This type of meditation is based on paying attention to the present moment without judgment. It can be practiced while doing yoga, walking, or eating, among other things.

Vipassana Meditation: This is the oldest form of Buddhist meditation and focus on the insight or inner understanding of the nature of reality and self.

Yoga Meditation: This form of meditation combines physical postures, breathing techniques, and focus on the present moment.

Loving-Kindness Meditation (Metta Meditation): This form of meditation focuses on developing feelings of love and compassion for oneself and others.

Chakra Meditation: This form of meditation focuses on the energy centers in the body called chakras.

Regardless of the technique, the goal of meditation and mindfulness practices is to achieve a state of inner peace and tranquility. In order to get the most out of these practices, it is recommended to find a quiet, comfortable place to meditate, set aside regular time for meditation, and practice regularly. With consistent practice and an open and curious mind, one can experience the benefits of meditation and mindfulness such as reduction of stress, anxiety, depression, and chronic pain, improvement of emotional well-being, increased focus and attention, and enhanced self-awareness.

Meditation and mindfulness are ancient techniques that have been used for centuries to cultivate inner peace and awareness. They involve training the mind to focus and become more aware of the present moment. There are many different types of meditation and mindfulness techniques, each with their own unique focus and benefits. They have been found to be beneficial for a wide range of physical and mental health conditions and can be practiced by anyone.

ᗑᗑᗑ

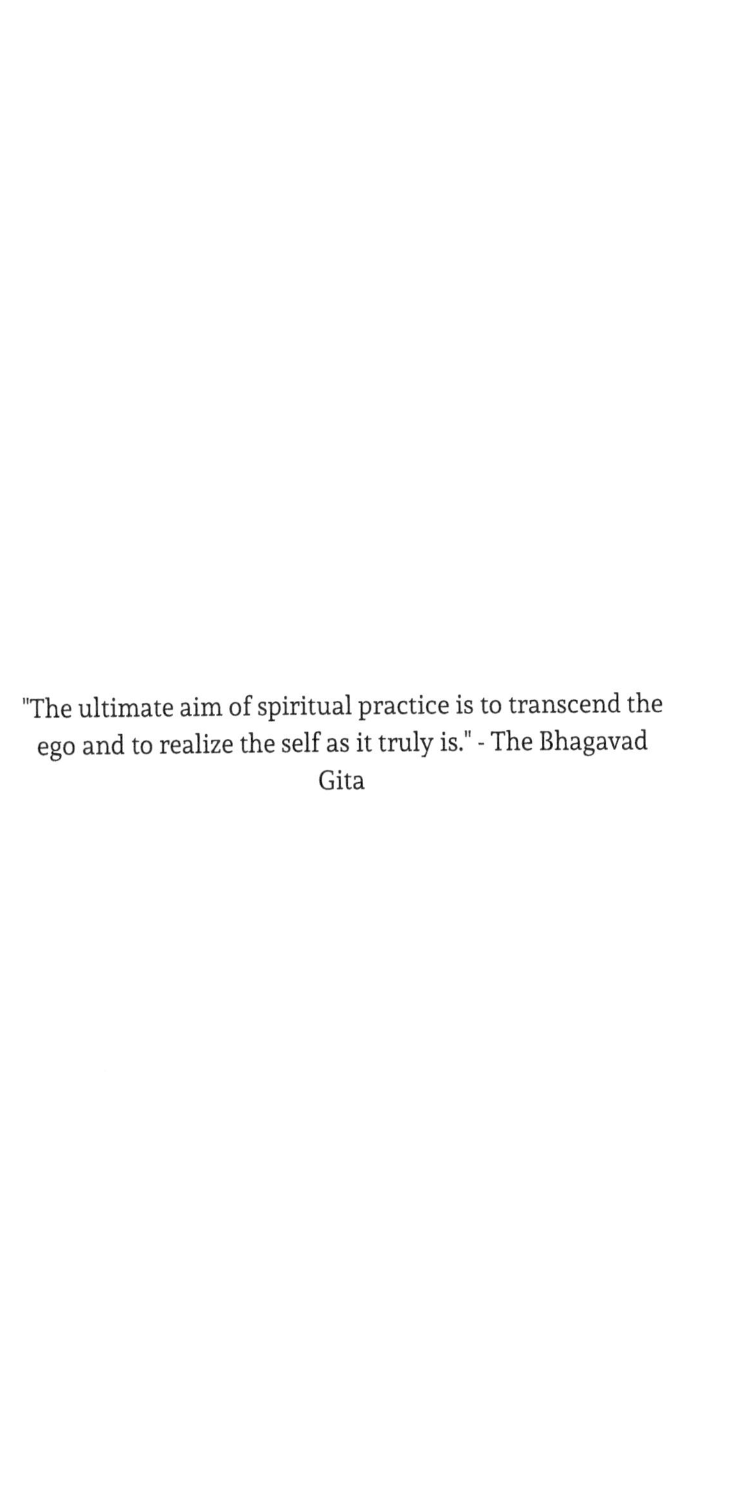

"The ultimate aim of spiritual practice is to transcend the ego and to realize the self as it truly is." - The Bhagavad Gita

TEN

FROM TEMPLES TO ASHRAMS: A GUIDE TO THE SACRED PLACES OF INDIAN SPIRITUALITY

India is a land of diverse spiritual traditions and is home to a wide variety of sacred places that have been central to the spiritual practices of millions of people over the centuries. These places range from grand temples and shrines to smaller ashrams and meditation centers. Each of these sacred places offers a unique perspective on Indian spirituality and culture, and they are an important part of the spiritual heritage of the country.

One of the most iconic sacred places in India is the temple. Temples are found all over the country and are dedicated to a wide range of Hindu deities. They are often grand and ornate structures, with intricate carvings and sculptures, and are considered to be powerful places of spiritual energy. Some of the most famous temples in India include the Meenakshi Temple in Madurai, the Virupaksha Temple in Hampi, and the Sri Ranganathaswamy Temple in Srirangam.

Another important sacred place in India is the Ashram. Ashrams are spiritual retreat centers where people come to live, study, and practice spiritual disciplines under the guidance of a spiritual teacher or guru. They often include facilities for meditation, yoga, and other spiritual practices, and provide an opportunity for people to study and explore spiritual teachings in a supportive and nurturing environment. Some of the most famous ashrams in India include the Sivananda Ashram in Rishikesh, the Aurobindo Ashram in Pondicherry, and the Isha Yoga Center in Coimbatore.

In addition to temples and ashrams, India is also home to many other sacred places such as Buddhist monasteries, Jain shrines, Sufi tombs and many other places that are considered holy. These places not only serve as important centers of spiritual practice and learning, but they also play an important role in the cultural heritage of India.

India is a land of diverse spiritual traditions and is home to a wide variety of sacred places that have been central to the spiritual practices of millions of people over the centuries. These places include grand temples and shrines, smaller ashrams and meditation centers, Buddhist monasteries, Jain shrines, Sufi tombs, and many other places that are considered holy. These sacred places offer a unique perspective on Indian spirituality and culture and they are an important part of the spiritual heritage of the country. They serve as important centers of spiritual practice and learning, and they also play an important role in the cultural heritage of India.

ᐅᐅᐅ

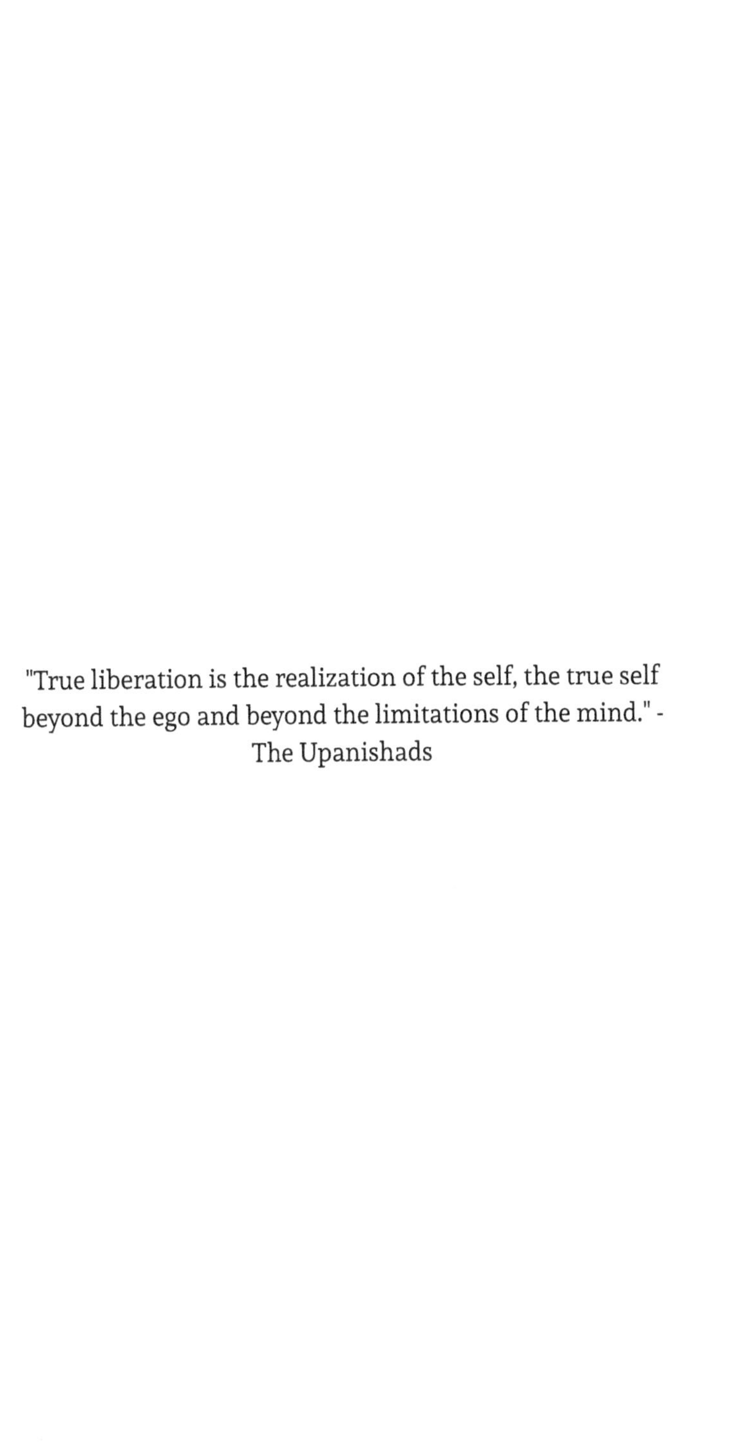

"True liberation is the realization of the self, the true self beyond the ego and beyond the limitations of the mind." - The Upanishads

ELEVEN

THE FUTURE OF INDIAN SPIRITUALITY: CONTEMPORARY TRENDS AND CHALLENGES

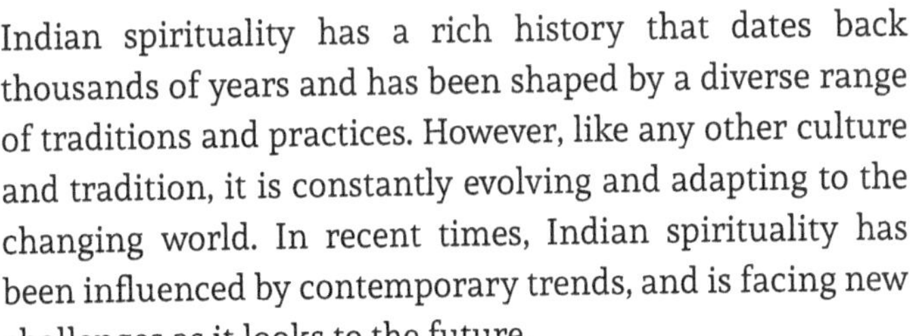

Indian spirituality has a rich history that dates back thousands of years and has been shaped by a diverse range of traditions and practices. However, like any other culture and tradition, it is constantly evolving and adapting to the changing world. In recent times, Indian spirituality has been influenced by contemporary trends, and is facing new challenges as it looks to the future.

One of the main trends that has been affecting Indian

spirituality in recent years is the growing popularity of yoga and meditation. Yoga has become a global phenomenon, and it is now considered to be one of the most popular forms of exercise and meditation in the world. This trend has led to the establishment of many yoga studios and retreat centers around the world and also many people are now practicing meditation and mindfulness as a daily routine.

Another trend that has been shaping the future of Indian spirituality is the increasing popularity of online and digital resources. With the widespread availability of the internet and smartphones, people have more access than ever before to spiritual teachings, practices, and communities. Websites, apps, social media platforms, and online forums have become important platforms for sharing spiritual knowledge and connecting with others who share similar interests and beliefs.

However, there are also some challenges that Indian spirituality is facing, one of them is the commercialization of spiritual practices and teachings. As the popularity of yoga, meditation, and other spiritual practices increases, it has also led to the commercialization of these practices, with some businesses and individuals looking to profit from the trend. This can lead to a loss of authenticity and a dilution of the original teachings and practices.

Another challenge is the commodification of spiritual traditions. Some spiritual traditions have been reduced to superficial experiences, and commercialized as exotic tourism experiences. This commodification of spiritual traditions can lead to a lack of respect and understanding of the culture and tradition that they come from, and can also lead to the erosion of the authenticity of these traditions.

Indian spirituality has a rich history and is constantly evolving, adapting to the changing world. In recent times, it has been influenced by contemporary trends such as the growing popularity of yoga and meditation, and the increasing popularity of online and digital resources. However, Indian spirituality also facing some challenges such as the commercialization and commodification of spiritual practices and teachings, which can lead to a loss of authenticity and dilution of original teachings and practices. It is important to maintain the balance between preserving traditional spiritual practices and teachings while embracing new and innovative ways to share and experience them in the modern world.

ၦၦၦ

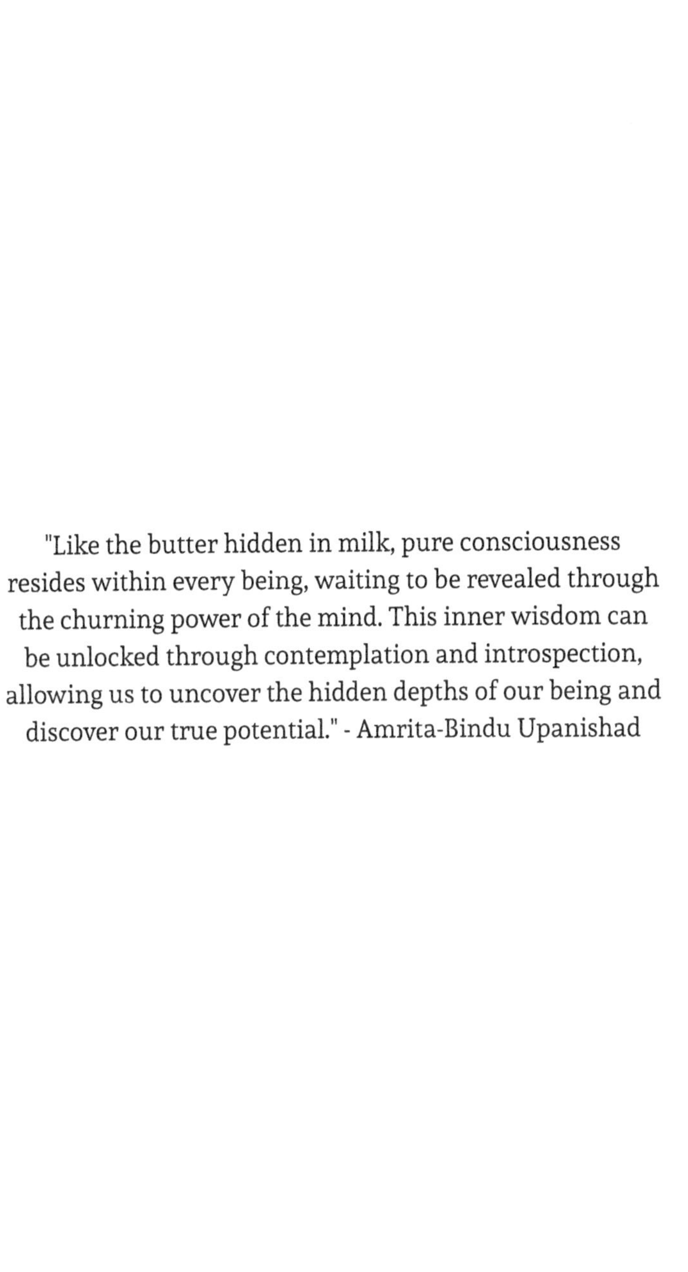

"Like the butter hidden in milk, pure consciousness resides within every being, waiting to be revealed through the churning power of the mind. This inner wisdom can be unlocked through contemplation and introspection, allowing us to uncover the hidden depths of our being and discover our true potential." - Amrita-Bindu Upanishad

TWELVE

RIVERS OF FAITH: THE SACRED RIVERS OF INDIA AND THEIR CONNECTION TO SPIRITUAL TRADITIONS AND BELIEFS

Rivers have played an important role in Indian spirituality, faith, and belief throughout history. Many rivers in India are considered sacred and are closely associated with various deities and spiritual traditions. These rivers are often the site of religious ceremonies, pilgrimage, and other rituals, and are considered to possess great spiritual power and significance. Some of the most significant rivers and how they are connected with Indian spirituality, faith and belief are:

Ganges: The Ganges, also known as the Ganga, is one of the most sacred rivers in India and is considered to be a goddess in her own right. It is believed to have the power to purify the souls of the deceased, and is the site of many religious ceremonies and rituals. Millions of Hindus make a pilgrimage to the Ganges each year to bathe in its waters and perform rituals in the hopes of purifying their souls.

Yamuna: The Yamuna is considered to be the sister river of the Ganges, and is considered to be a manifestation of the goddess Yamuna. It is also an important site of pilgrimage and ritual, with many temples and shrines located along its banks.

Narmada: The Narmada is considered to be one of the seven holiest rivers in India and is revered as a goddess. It is the site of many religious ceremonies and rituals, and is also an important destination for pilgrimage.

Godavari: The Godavari is considered to be one of the most sacred rivers in South India, it is believed to have originated from the locks of Lord Brahma and is considered to be a goddess herself. It is a site of many religious ceremonies, and is also an important destination for pilgrimage.

Kaveri: The Kaveri is considered to be one of the most sacred rivers in South India, it is also considered to be a goddess and has many shrines and temples located along its banks. It is believed to be a source of fertility and prosperity, and many rituals are performed to appease the river goddess.

These are just a few examples of the rivers in India that are considered to be sacred and are closely associated with spiritual traditions and beliefs. These rivers are a source of spiritual inspiration and devotion, and they continue to play an important role in Indian spirituality, culture, and tradition.

Rivers have played an important role in Indian spirituality, faith, and belief throughout history, many rivers in India are considered sacred and closely associated with various deities and spiritual traditions. Rivers like Ganges, Yamuna, Narmada, Godavari, Kaveri are some of the most significant rivers and are considered as powerful sources of spiritual energy and are deeply connected with various religious and spiritual practices and beliefs. These rivers are often the site of religious ceremonies, pilgrimage, and other rituals, and many people believe that bathing in the waters of these rivers and performing other rituals has the power to purify the soul and bring blessings, prosperity, and fertility. These rivers are also considered as goddesses and many shrines and temples are located along their banks, these rivers are considered as a means to connect with the divine and attain spiritual liberation. They continue to play an important role in Indian spirituality, culture and tradition, and hold an important place in the hearts of millions of people.

ﭘﭘﭘ

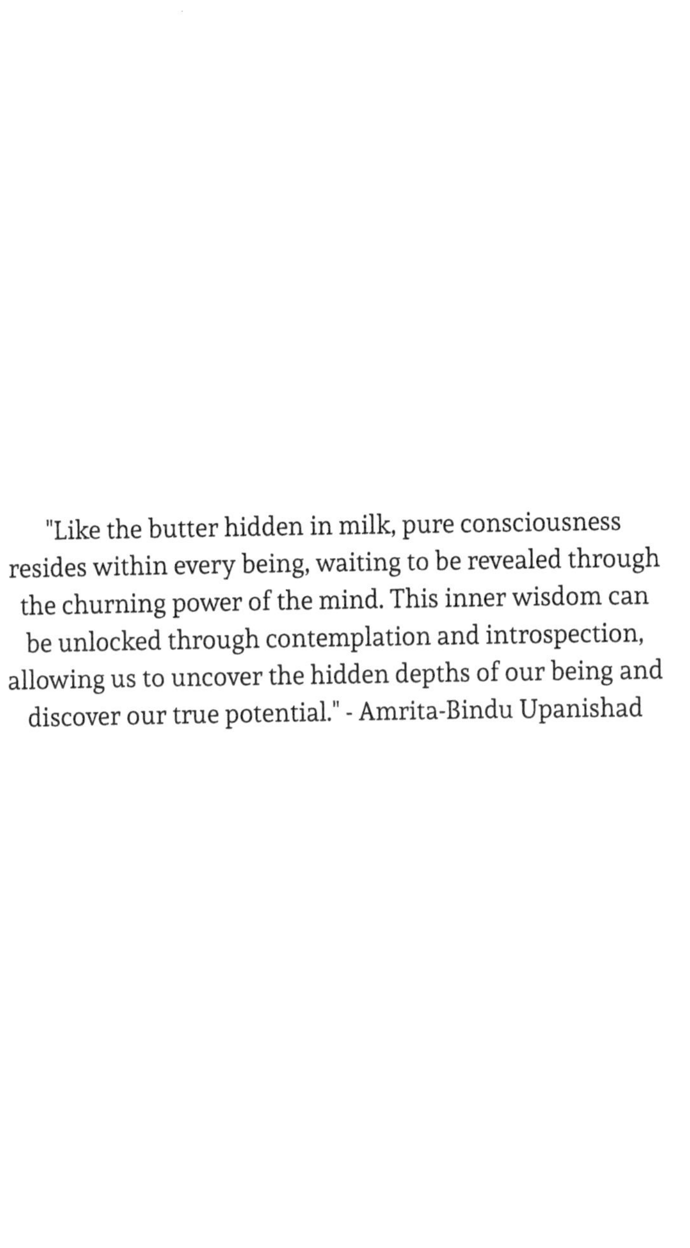

"Like the butter hidden in milk, pure consciousness resides within every being, waiting to be revealed through the churning power of the mind. This inner wisdom can be unlocked through contemplation and introspection, allowing us to uncover the hidden depths of our being and discover our true potential." - Amrita-Bindu Upanishad

THIRTEEN

QUOTES FROM INDIAN SCRIPTURES

The Vedas and Upanishads are ancient texts and scriptures that have been used for centuries to explain the depths of Indian spirituality. In these texts, all the major spiritual beliefs, philosophies and practices of Indian religion have been immortalized in the form of quotes. Here, we shall delve into some of the most profound and enlightening quotes on Indian spirituality found in Vedas and Upanishads.

The first quote is from the Chandogya Upanishad, which speaks of the ultimate unity of all beings: "One becomes flawless by perceiving the Self as radiant and whole. Indeed, all things have the same origin." This is a reminder that, despite our outer differences, everything in the universe is ultimately connected. We are all composed of the same energy and are all fundamentally one.

The next famous quote is by the ancient sage Yajnavalkya, which originates from the Brihadaranyaka Upanishad. He states: "The Self is smaller than the smallest, and greater than the greatest." By comparing the Self to both the small and great, Yagnavalkya conveys the mysterious power of the Self which can never be fully understood. It is incredibly vast and yet incredibly small, beyond the grasp of words and logic.

The Rig Veda contains many timeless quotes that speak of the power and importance of spiritual practices. One such quote states: "Let a man meditate upon his own Self as his most exalted object; for the knowledge of the Self is the highest knowledge." This emphasizes the value of self-reflection and meditation in helping one to understand oneself more deeply and to gain knowledge of their true nature.

Finally, another profound and deeply spiritual quote comes from the Isha Upanishad: "The Lord is subtler than the subtlest, and greater than the greatest. He is hidden in all beings and is all-pervading." This quote speaks of the all-encompassing and ineffable nature of God, which is both mysterious and pervasive. It also reminds us that God is ever-present, and that no matter where we go or what we do, He is there with us.

These quotes from Vedas and Upanishad, taken together, provide timeless wisdom on Indian spirituality and its many diverse pathways. They remind us of the unity and oneness of existence, the power of the Self, the importance of spiritual practice, and the presence of God in all.

❦❦❦

To revere our mothers, fathers, teachers, and guests as divine beings is a sacred act. We can honor them by treating them with the utmost respect and admiration, as if they were gods. Doing so is a way of expressing our gratitude for all that they have done for us. It is also a way of showing our appreciation for the wisdom and guidance they have provided us. By treating them with reverence, we can demonstrate our commitment to upholding the highest standards of morality and integrity. - The Taittiriya Upanishad

FOURTEEN
SUMMARY

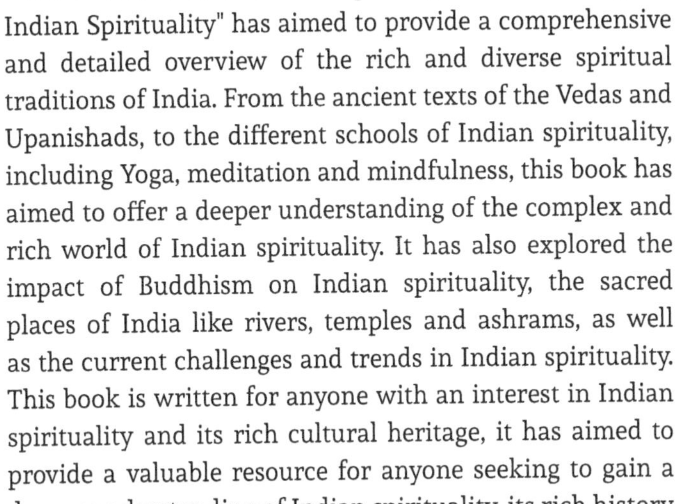

"Echoes of Ancient Wisdom: Exploring the Rich Heritage of Indian Spirituality" has aimed to provide a comprehensive and detailed overview of the rich and diverse spiritual traditions of India. From the ancient texts of the Vedas and Upanishads, to the different schools of Indian spirituality, including Yoga, meditation and mindfulness, this book has aimed to offer a deeper understanding of the complex and rich world of Indian spirituality. It has also explored the impact of Buddhism on Indian spirituality, the sacred places of India like rivers, temples and ashrams, as well as the current challenges and trends in Indian spirituality. This book is written for anyone with an interest in Indian spirituality and its rich cultural heritage, it has aimed to provide a valuable resource for anyone seeking to gain a deeper understanding of Indian spirituality, its rich history and its ongoing relevance in today's world. It is our hope that this book will have served as an inspiration and guide for readers on their journey of self-discovery and spiritual development.

Victory is destined for those brave and honest enough to adhere to truth - Mundaka Upanishad

Other Books Of The Author

1. The Moments When I Met God
2. Kashiyile Theertha Pathangal
3. GURU GYAN VANI
4. Abhiprerak Gita
5. ASSI SE JAIN GHAT TAK
6. Hopelessness of Arjuna
7. The Soul and It's True Nature
8. Sense of Action (Karma)
9. Action through Wisdom
10. Action through Wisdom
11. THEORY AND PRACTICAL OF EVERY ACTION
12. LOGICAL UNDERSTANDING OF THE SUPREME
13. THE IMPERISHABLE SUPREME
14. Yatra Nishadraj se Hanuman Ghat Tak
15. Yatra Karnatak Ghat se Raja Ghat Tak
16. Yatra Pandey Ghat se Prayagraj Ghat Tak
17. Yatra Ranjendra Prasad Ghat se Dattatreya Ghat Tak
18. YaatraSindhiya Ghat se Gwaliar Ghat Tak
19. Yatra Mangala Gauri Ghat se Hanuman Gadhi Ghat Tak
20. Yatra Gaay Ghat Se Nishad Ghat Tak
21. MAA GANGA, GHATEN EVM UTSAV
22. Ganga Arti Dev Deepavali evam Any Utsav
23. Potentials of Digitalized India
24. VEDIC CONSCIOUSNESS
25. A Brief Introduction to Vedic Science
26. Kashi ke Barah Jyotirling
27. IMPACT OF MOTIVATION
28. Let's have a Milky Way Journey
29. Color Therapy in a Nutshell

30. Rigveda in a Nutshell
31. Yajurveda in a Nutshell
32. Samveda in a Nutshell
33. Atharva Veda in a Nutshell
34. Ayushman Bhava - Ayurveda
35. Srimad Bhagavad Gita and Upanishad Connection
36. Srimad Bhagavad Gita - an attempt to summarize each chapter.
37. Facts and Impact of Nakshatra
38. Astro Gems - NAVARATNA
39. Ekadashi - A Concise Overview
40. A Concise View of Hanuman Chalisa
41. Inspirational Gita
42. Nakshatraranyam
43. Summary of 18 Mahapuranas
44. Synopsis of 18 Upa Puranas
45. Rigvediya Upanishads
46. Shukla Yajurvediya Upanishads
47. Krishna Yajurvediya Upanishads
48. Samavediya Upanishads
49. Atharvavediya Upanishads
50. The Seven Great Sages
51. From Rocket Scientist to President Dr. APJ Abdul Kalam
52. The Visionary's Voice - Quotes of Dr. APJ Abdul Kalam
53. The Wisdom of Swami Vivekananda: Insights and Inspiration from a Legendary Spiritual Teacher
54. Ayurvedic Remedies from the Garden
55. Sages and Seers
56. Rising Strong – Motivational Stories of Women
57. Beyond Flames -Mystery stories of Funeral Ghat Manikarnika
58. The Origins of Tulsi: A Look at the Mythological Roots of the Plant"

59. The Holistic Cow: A Look at the Physical, Spiritual, and Cultural Importance of Cows in India
60. Arts of Healing
61. Exploring the Divine
62. Understanding Five Elements
63. The Etymology of Ram
64. Symbols of India
65. Voice of Change (About Speeches of Great Men)
66. She Speaks (About Speeches of Great Women)
67. Patriotism on Celluloid – Brief About Patriotic Films
68. The Music of Motivation: A Brief Guide to Inspirational Film Songs
69. Unlocking the Secrets of the Dashopanishads
70. Echoes of Ancient Wisdom: Exploring the Rich Heritage of Indian Spirituality

ϷϷϷ

Contact

DR. JAGADEESH PILLAI

PhD in Vedic Science

Four Times Guinness World Record Holder

Winner of Mahatma Gandhi Vishwa Shanti Puraskar and Global Peace Ambassador

Gemology, Astro & Vastu Consultant - Spiritual Counselor

Consultant for designing World Record Ideas

Efficient Tarot Card Reader

9839093003

myrichindia@gmail.com

drjagadeeshpillai@facebook

drjagadeeshpillai@instagram

jagadeeshpillai@youtube

www. JAGADEESHPILLAI.com

|| LOKAHA SAMASTHAHA SUKHINO BHAVANTU ||